For Cara
who loves animals of all kinds—
with all my love

Polly Vaughn

A TRADITIONAL BRITISH BALLAD
DESIGNED, ILLUSTRATED, AND
RETOLD IN AN AMERICAN
SETTING BY

Barry Moser

Little, Brown and Company
Boston   Toronto   London

First Edition

Library of Congress Cataloging-in-Publication Data

Moser, Barry.
   Polly Vaughn: a traditional British ballad / designed, illustrated, and
retold in an American setting by Barry Moser. — 1st ed.
      p.   cm.
   Summary: Inspired by a traditional English ballad, this tragedy
set in the deep South of the U.S. features two sweethearts whose
love is interrupted by a hunting accident.
   ISBN 0-316-58541-6
   1. Ballads, English — South (U.S.) — Texts.   [1. Ballads, English —
South (U.S.)]   I. Title.
PZ8.3.M8434Po   1992
[398.2] — dc20   91-2994
                              NIL

                  10 9 8 7 6 5 4 3 2 1

          Published simultaneously in Canada
       by Little, Brown & Company (Canada) Limited

                     Printed in Italy

Polly Vaughn

Frontispiece: Polly, aged fifteen, with her favorite hen, Birdie Mae.

*P*OLLY AND JIMMY WERE SWEETHEARTS. Had been since they were kids in "kinleygarten." All the boys liked Polly. The girls did, too. But of all her friends Polly liked Jimmy Randall best. And he liked her best. She called him "Jimmer" and he called her "Pol." They were sweethearts up to the tenth grade, when Jimmy quit school to go to work in the coal mines. They were sweethearts after that, too, and were to be married on Polly's twentieth birthday, which was two weeks away.

Polly and her mother were making dresses and were busy sewing and trying them on. Polly looked pretty in her white dress, even though there was nothing special about her looks except a quick, warm smile and her long, fawn-colored hair. It was her kind nature and generous spirit that everybody loved so much. "She's such a *sweet* chile," was what everybody said about her. She was as kind and sweet to strangers and animals as she was to her own family. She loved animals of all kinds. She brought home sick and hurt animals so often that her mother would say, "I declare, that chile loves animals more than she does folks."

Polly and her family lived halfway up Cold Iron Mountain in a cabin that had been in her family for four generations. Polly's daddy, Merle Vaughn, worked in the Stone Creek Mines just like his daddy and granddaddy had. He

◄ *Polly and Jimmy in the second grade, the day before school let out for the summer.*

stayed inside most all the time — inside the mines, inside the house, and inside himself. Polly's momma, Bessie Joyce, was a stout woman, and real talkative. She and Polly talked all the time — about what book Polly was reading and about the wedding and about the cabin Polly and Jimmy were planning to build. Every year Bessie Joyce put in a truck garden that was as pretty as a picture. She looked after the cows and pigs, too, and raised all the children — Polly and her two brothers and three sisters: Lottie and Anna Belle, Truman and John Delmar, and the baby, Florinda.

Jimmy was a sweet kid, too, and most everybody liked him. He had always been shy and, like Polly, nothing special to look at. He had a shock of red hair and a mess of freckles all over his nose. As a boy he liked to play softball and he liked to shoot marbles. He played ball with the boys, but he shot marbles with Polly. He'd just smile and go on about his business when the boys kidded him for playing with Polly. But she could shoot Rolley Hole better than any of them — and besides that, she had her own bag of flint marbles.

Even when they weren't in school, Polly and Jimmy spent a lot of time together — swinging in the swing on Polly's front porch, shooting Rolley Hole, or playing Old Maid. Most of all, though, they walked in the woods together. Polly wasn't afraid of snakes or lizards or tadpoles or anything. She'd go places he wouldn't go, she saw things that he didn't see, and she knew things he didn't know — the names of plants and animals and birds and insects. She even knew which mushrooms and roots you could eat. Jimmy's folks didn't eat things like that — they ate pork and venison, corn and collard greens, and potatoes and johnnycake.

Jimmy's folks kept pretty much to themselves. When the Randalls moved to Cold Iron Mountain, back in 1907, Merle Vaughn claimed that the Randalls had gone and built their cabin on Vaughn land. There was a big dispute, and Merle nailed a sign up in the woods warning "all Randalls and all other liars" not to set foot on his land, else he'd shoot them. Merle Vaughn had held a grudge against the Randalls ever since.

◀ *Even though Merle Vaughn held an old family grudge against Jimmy, his wife, Bessie Joyce, was fond of the boy.*

Jewett Randall worked in the Stone Creek Mines, too, though nowhere near Merle Vaughn. The only friends Jewett Randall had were his family. He was an irascible man, Jewett — always a bad mood, always a mean tongue, and always quick to fight. Some said that they believed old Jewett kind of liked the dispute over the land. Said it "give him something to be mad about" all the time. Then again, Jewett didn't like people any better than they liked him. About the only things he did like were his family and hunting, and, my, how that man loved hunting — rabbits, wild turkeys, black bears, partridges, pigeons — it didn't matter to Jewett Randall what he hunted or where he hunted it. Deer hunting, though, was special in the Randall family. Like in most of the families on Cold Iron Mountain, it was a way of life. It was what they talked about sitting on the porch. It was what they talked about sitting at the dinner table. It was what they talked about sitting around the fire.

Jimmy was ten when he killed his first deer, a doe. It was early spring, out of season. Jimmy didn't even want to go that morning. He was going over to play with Polly, but his daddy and his brother, Lester, teased him about playing with girls, so Jimmy went along. There were patches of snow still hiding behind rocks and beneath trees, and when the doe sprang over the fence, Jimmy saw her white tail flash in the morning sunlight. He pointed his gun and shot — not thinking, really, just hoping to please his daddy and impress his big brother. It wasn't a clean shot. She fell into the fence and tangled her hind leg in the barbed wire. Jimmy had to shoot her again, up close, to put her out of her misery. Jimmy hated that. His daddy told him it was all right, "'cause it had to be done," and anyway, he said, "a doe tastes jest as good as a buck does. It's jest too bad ya shot when ya did, son, 'cause yer brother Lester here had a big eight-point buck in his sights jest as ya fired, and he done got away clean. Boy! Them antlers shore would've looked mighty han'some over the mantelpiece." Jewett and Lester hung the doe by her hocks on a meat pole and tried to get Jimmy to gut her, but Jimmy wouldn't do it. So his daddy did it for him. And when he did, the doe's entrails spilled out warm and steaming on the cold

◄ *The doe that Jimmy mistook for a buck on Jedediah Coover's land.*

ground. Jewett cupped his hand in some of her blood and smeared it on Jimmy's face. That's what men do to celebrate a boy's first kill. To Jewett and Lester, Jimmy was a man. But Jimmy didn't feel any different — all he felt was a little sick to his stomach. Jimmy never cared for hunting after that.

Merle Vaughn said he wasn't going to go to the wedding, but Polly and her mama weren't concerned — they figured he'd change his mind. They were happy and excited as they put the final touches of lace on Polly's dress. That afternoon, when they finished, Polly went out for a walk in the woods. She pulled on a pair of old coveralls — right over her favorite blouse, a white cotton one with a lace collar. Polly loved lace. She had taught herself to make "poor man's lace" years ago when she had chicken pox and had to stay home from school for two weeks. She had tatted a good deal of it for her wedding dress. When she left the house she put on a buckskin jacket that Jimmy's mother, Eulalia, had made for her from the hide of a deer that Jimmy's brother had killed. Polly didn't like it that the Randalls hunted deer; she was glad that her daddy and brothers and Jimmy didn't like hunting. Jimmy had told Polly that all he liked about hunting was getting out in the woods with his family and friends. He told her that sometimes he'd shoot wide, missing his target on purpose, and that sometimes he'd shoot at nothing at all just to scare things away — except, of course, when the family needed something to eat. Nonetheless, Polly was glad she had the jacket on because it was warm and it protected her lace from prickers and thorns.

Jimmy was in the woods, too, that November afternoon. He was taking a shortcut over to the Vaughn place to meet Polly and go to Sunday evening prayer meeting with her. He had gone only a few feet from the cabin when his mama hollered at him: "Take yer gun with ya, Jimmy — jest in case ya see som'thin', honey — God knows we shore could use some fresh meat." So Jimmy went back to the cabin and fetched his gun.

◀ *Jimmy in the woods with his grandfather's gun, "Old Neverfail."*

He was nearing the old Wilhoit Bridge when he heard something rustling in the bushes on the other side of the creek.

Polly was gathering gentian when she heard footsteps in the fallen leaves.

Jimmy, being as quiet as he could, made his way through the underbrush till he came round under the bridge. A stone plunked into the water.

The flounce of lace danced at Polly's neck as she stood up and turned toward the sound. She saw Jimmy through the trees.

Jimmy saw the flash of white. He pointed his gun and shot.

Polly fell.

The echo of the shot reverberated through the stand of yellow birches as a circle of smoke curled upward into the trees and lost its shape.

He ran and the forest floor crunched underfoot. Then he saw — not the fine buck he thought he had shot — but Polly. He dropped his gun to the ground and fell to his knees beside her. Her white lace was spattered with blood. She looked at Jimmy. Her breathing was faint and unsteady. Horrified and shaking, he lifted her head and cradled it in his lap. A single word whispered from her sweet mouth — "Jimmer."

Jimmy rocked back and forth, hugging her head to his chest. He tasted the salt of his tears when he said, "You'll be all right, sweetheart. I swear. You'll be okay. I'll git help — the house's just over yonder, Pol . . . oh, Polly, Polly."

Jimmy lifted Polly in his arms and carried her toward the cabin, her face snuggled to his chest. Her arm drooped toward the ground and the gentian fell from her hand.

Jimmy staggered up onto the porch, kissing Polly's head and sobbing, "You're jest hurt, sweetheart, jest hurt a little, that's all. Mama'll fix ya up." It was his mama who first said that no, she wasn't hurt, she was dead. She made Jimmy lay Polly on the divan in front of the fireplace, saying, "Land sakes, boy, try to get aholt of yerself." Jewett Randall grabbed Jimmy's shoulders and turned him around and asked him how this had happened. Jimmy told him — as best he could. But it was hard. He didn't want to admit that his precious

◄ *Polly's lace collar stained with blood as she fell.*

Polly was dead — that he had shot her just like he had shot that doe ten years ago. Then Jewett said, "Son, we gotta go tell Merle and Bessie Joyce about this, jest quick's we can. It's goin' be real hard on 'em. Ain't no tellin' what ol' Merle's like to do." Jimmy nodded in agreement. Then Jewett turned to Lester and told him to go get the truck and drive over to the Vaughn place and fetch Merle. Doing as he was told, Lester stopped by the front door, put on his coat and hat, and picked up his gun. Jewett warned him to be careful.

A little later Lester's truck skidded to a stop back in front of the Randall cabin. Doors opened and slammed. Lester and Merle came rushing up onto the porch. Merle bolted through the door and when he saw Polly, he stiffened — straight as a poker. Merle was no stranger to death. He had seen a lot of it in the mines. Had nearly died a few times himself. Jewett and Lester could see the muscles in his cheeks flex.

Then Merle turned, slowly, and faced Jimmy, and with hate and anger trembling in his voice, he said, "You done this, didn't ya?" He drew back his hand to hit Jimmy, but Lester stepped in between them. Jimmy turned and walked out of the cabin and into the cold November dusk. His face was stained with tears and his throat was swollen shut with grief. He walked in a blur back to the Wilhoit Bridge. He found his gun where he had dropped it, and in a fit of rage he smashed it again and again against a tree, then hurled it, bent and splintered, into the creek.

Polly was buried a week later, on the very day she and Jimmy were to have been married. Reverend Carlester Devore started preaching a sermon about goodness and innocence and love. "Love is like the mawnin' an' the evenin' star," he began. He went on and on, about this and that, till a faint drizzle started up and forced him to quit — but not before reminding everyone about the fellowship pancake supper at the Nine Mile Baptist Church later that evening. Jimmy and his family were leaving the cemetery, heading over to their truck,

◀ *Jewett and Eulalia Randall confront the arriving Vaughns.*

when the sheriff, Hoyt Clepper, came up to Jimmy, put his hand on his shoulder, and said, "Son, I hate like the very dickens to have to do this, but . . . I gotta put ya under arrest for the murder of Miss Polly."

"Murder?" Jimmy protested. "Murder? Mr. Clepper, I loved her. She was my whole life. It was an accident. You must know that. An accident, a terrible accident. I thought I saw a deer. I thought she was a deer!" But Sheriff Clepper, as he was putting handcuffs on Jimmy's wrists, said, "Son, I'm sorry. I believe ya, but old Merle Vaughn there has brought this here charge agin' ya and there ain't nothin' I can do about it. Anyway, I don't really think nothin'll come of it."

The drizzle turned to rain as Sheriff Clepper put Jimmy in the Model A and drove off down the gravel road toward the county seat.

They put Jimmy on a chain gang where he worked all day raking the courthouse lawn and fixing potholes in the roads all around Baldwin County. His family visited him when they could and brought him food — fried okra and turnip greens, johnnycake and smothered porkchops — all Jimmy's favorites, but Jimmy couldn't eat. Reverend Devore brought Jimmy a floppy little Bible and prayed with him and talked to him about salvation and forgiveness, and trusting in God. But Jimmy didn't hear. He did read the Bible some, though — after Reverend Devore left — and when he read that love bears all things and endures all things and that love never ends, he just leaned back and stared at the stains and peeling plaster on the ceiling of his cell, yearning for Polly. Polly. Oh, God, if only his mama hadn't hollered at him, if only he'd not gone back for that gun, that damned gun.

Despite the hard work of the chain gang, Jimmy couldn't sleep. He lay awake night after night, staring at the ceiling and thinking about Polly. Then, on the night before his trial, as Jimmy was lying on his cot, the stains on the ceiling began to move and to take shapes — shapes of strange animals — deer with tusks and turkeys with horns and boars with wings. And then the animals dissolved. And in their place he saw Polly — in a soft light — and he heard her

◀ *Sheriff Hoyt Clepper at Polly's funeral dreading what he has to do.*

voice: "Jimmer," her voice said lovingly, "don't you fret about tomorrow, sweetheart. You tell those men the truth. You tell them that it was an accident, and you tell them that you loved me. You tell them the truth, Jimmer. And remember that I love you and that I'll always love you, my dear, dear Jimmer. Our love will make everything right. I promise."

The next morning, Sheriff Clepper found Jimmy sleeping peacefully.

It was snowing outside the courthouse where Judge Harland T. Slaymaker was bringing the court to order. Harland T. Slaymaker didn't like long trials, especially during hunting season, and over the years, because of his hurried manner of dispatching cases, he had come to be known as "High Gear Harland."

The jurors were all men. Jimmy knew them and they knew Jimmy. They knew his daddy, too. And they knew the story of Jimmy's first kill, and they believed that they were stronger men than Jimmy. They believed that they were better hunters, too, and that they were incapable of such a mistake.

Polly's father was the first to take the stand.

His voice was slow and cold when he told the judge and jury that it "warn't no accident. Yer Honner, I tell you it warn't like that boy sez. Couldn't've been. I tell ya he'uz too close to her not to 'uv seen her good. Thay'uz all crazy, them Randalls — him an' his daddy and that ugly brother of his, too. That boy done killed my little girl." Merle Vaughn's voice became a whisper when he said, finally, "Jimmy Randall murdered my Polly."

Jedediah Coover took the stand next. He started testifying and raving and pointing his cane at Jimmy before the clerk could swear him in. "Ya gotta sit down an' get swore in first, Jedediah, then ya kin speak yer piece," the judge said. Jedediah settled down and took his oath and started right in accusing the Randalls of poaching game on his property and of shooting one of his cows and two of his coon dogs. He said they killed his dog, Jojo, because "Jojo wuz a-chasin' a deer they 'uz a-huntin'. A-huntin' on my own property, too, Judge."

◀ *Judge Harland T. Slaymaker was impatient with carelessness and long trials.*

Even though Jedediah had no proof of this, the jurors believed it because they wanted to believe it.

Nobody testified on Jimmy's behalf. Bessie Joyce Vaughn wanted to speak up for him, but Merle wouldn't let her — told her to sit quiet and hold her peace. So, when it came time, Jimmy took the stand on his own behalf. He told the court that it was an accident, that though it was Polly's lace he saw, he thought it was the tail of a deer. He told them that he couldn't see Polly because of the underbrush between him and her. He admitted being careless and stupid and too anxious to please his family. And then he told the judge and the jury what Polly told him to say, being careful, though, not to say that Polly came to him in a dream. That'd be too much like a ghost story, and these men would never believe anything like that — especially Harland T. Slaymaker and Carlester Devore. Jimmy's testimony turned bright, almost happy, when he talked about Polly and how much he loved her, and when he finished he thought everything would be all right. He thought the jury believed him.

The jurors retired to the jury room to deliberate and came back ten minutes later. Reverend Carlester Devore, the foreman, was the last one back in. When the room was quiet, Judge Slaymaker asked for the verdict. Reverend Devore stood up and leaned forward against the banister of the jury box, all pious and solemn, and with an air of self-importance, pronounced, in his deepest preacher's voice, "Guilty, yer Honner. Guilty of murder."

On the word "murder," a rage of wind slammed open the courtroom doors. The framed portrait of George Washington fell off the wall and crashed to the floor. Dead leaves and curtains of snow blew down the aisle of the courtroom. Bitter wind blew bonnets off women's heads and danced them in the air for a moment, along with the papers off the judge's desk and John Austin Chambers's hairpiece. Then, just as suddenly, the doors slammed shut. The flag by the judge's sidebar, which had been blowing wildly, now fluttered for a moment and became still. In front of the jury box a single veil of snow swirled and billowed like lace in an open window. The jurors, their hair blown

◄ *Reverend Carlester Devore gives the verdict. Weldon Twyner and Dewitt Bodfish approve.*

and their teeth chattering, looked at each other nervously. The snow-lace wafted gracefully in the dark, chilled courtroom air. A moment later it began to change shape, taking on a form like a pale and translucent young woman.

Then a voice, cold and transparent like the air itself, said, "You judge my Jimmer wrongly. Don't forget — you taught him that hunting is a badge of manhood, you smeared his face with the blood of a doe. My death was an accident. Jimmer loves me, and I love Jimmer. Please judge him fairly."

The doors to the courtroom blew open again. Leaves and snow again filled the air as the veil of snow-lace disappeared through the open doors.

The doors slammed shut.

All was still for a while. Faces were pale. Skin was gooseflesh. Voices were quiet. Then, a low prattle started up among the jurors and among the people in the courtroom. Reverend Devore looked at his brother, Holmes R., in disbelief, and said "There ain't no such thangs as ghosts!" Weldon Twyner, Fulton Upkins, and Dewitt Bodfish huddled together and resolved not to believe what they had just seen. The others just sat still, eyes wide open, staring straight ahead. All except for old Jedediah Coover, who clambered to his feet, exclaiming, "This here's some kinda trick! It's some kinda trick I tell ya, a trick ol' Jewett Randall cooked up to save his boy and to keep us from doin' what's right. I, fer one, ain't goin' to be turned around by no galdarned carnival trick."

"Hear, hear!" shouted Edmirl Stubblefield. Others joined in. "Hear, hear."

"Hang him," shouted John Austin Chambers, pulling himself to his feet and brandishing his cane above his head.

Judge Slaymaker picked up his gavel and brought it down sharply, again and again, shouting over the tumult, "Order! Order! Order in the court!"

The room got quiet. Old John Austin Chambers remained standing, his toothless mouth pouting and sucking, his eyes darting from one face to another, looking for approval. "Sit down, John Austin," Judge Slaymaker said indulgently, taking his spectacles off his nose. John Austin sat down, slowly. The judge looked at the jury. Some of them sat as still as could be, some stared

◀ *In the veil of snow Polly's eyes shone clearly.*

at their folded hands, some fidgeted, and some crossed their arms across their chests and looked smug. A few moments passed in silence. Then Judge Slaymaker put his glasses back on his nose and appeared to be studying the scattered papers left on his desk. Finally he looked sternly over his spectacles and said, "The jury has spoken." He was quiet for a moment, then continued, "I sentence you to be hanged by the neck until you are dead."

A hush fell across the room. Eulalia Randall burst into tears. Lester and Jewett consoled her. "Sentence to be carried out one week from today at ten o'clock in the morning." He hammered down the gavel sharply, pushed his chair back from his desk, and walked briskly to his chambers.

The Randalls went home. Lester took the truck and drove off. Eulalia put on her apron, thinking she'd make some johnnycake, but she just leaned against the sink and stared out the window at the snow turning to rain. Jewett sat by the fire and cleaned his gun. When he finished, he hung it over the mantelpiece and never took it down again.

The next week Jimmy was set astride a horse and led to an old catalpa tree on the outskirts of town. A small crowd had gathered, mostly men. Some curious children were there, too, all bundled up, running around, squealing, and hiding behind wagons and trees, hoping nobody would see them and run them away. A few speckled chickens squawked and clucked alongside the road, pecking at each other and at specks in the snow. A pair of old hound dogs had run a squirrel up the tree and were dancing on their hind legs, barking at it. Old John Austin Chambers had pushed his way to the front of the gathering, whipping people aside with his cane. Reverend Devore stood next to him with his eyes closed and his head bowed, caressing his Bible. Judge Slaymaker stood in front dressed in black. Jimmy wore only a light jacket and was shivering from the cold and fear. A gentle wind blew snow in drifts and into delicate eddies. Sheriff Clepper stood on the back of his Model A and looped the noose around Jimmy's neck. It was heavy and rough.

◄ *A light snow fell as Fulton Upkins prepared the rope.*

Then, without warning, the wind gusted and howled. The old catalpa
swayed and moaned. Snow blew up from the ground in sheets
and whirlwinds. And later, when the story was told,
some said that just as the sheriff slapped
the horse on her flank, the snow
swirled about Jimmy and
embraced him like
a shroud of
cold, white lace.

Afterword

So come all you bold sportsmen that carry a gun
I will have you go home by the light of the sun

So begins the traditional ballad of "Polly Vaughn" in one of its many extant forms. Like all folk ballads, it is a story about ordinary people in everyday situations. Its plot is based on local lore and topical events, much like a local newspaper or national tabloid. And like most folk ballads, it deals with a family tragedy. Ballads about tragedies between strangers are rare, and comic ballads are practically nonexistent.

"Polly Vaughn" is in the tradition of ballads that sing of true love. Like "Barbara Allen," "The Cruel Brother," and "The Unquiet Grave," it is also in the tradition of ballads that end in death. And like "The Wife of Usher's Well," "Sir Patrick Spens," and "Lord Randall My Son," it is in the tradition of ballads that not only tell tales of ghosts, but present the idea that if one has direct contact with the dead, as Jimmy did with Polly, the dead will take care of the living.

Storytelling, for me, springs from childhood. Not so much from remembering things I did and saw, but from remembering the voices of my relatives — the voice of an aunt or an uncle, or a distant cousin from over in Decherd — telling stories, to me and to one another, about the people who lived in "the hollow," or up Rockway Drive, or across the street. I hear my daddy telling stories on our Sunday afternoon rides over to Copper Hill or down to Sand Mountain, and if our ride happened to bring us home after dark along Shallowford Road, he would tell us his tale about a "headless haint" who haunted the road where it passed through a dark stretch of woods and would fly into our headlights "like a sheet." Because Shallowford Road was the road we lived on, his story was all the more frightening.

I hear "Polly Vaughn" in a more recent voice, too. It is the voice of a hunter, a young man dressed in a shock of orange, who came up to me out of the woods around my home, saying "Hey, mister! You know, you oughta keep your dogs tied up during deer season. Not that I'd shoot a dog or anything, but I know a lot of guys that would."

The tragedy of Polly Vaughn has been sung for generations in England and Ireland. My telling of it is a variation on an ancient theme — an American variation, as it were, woven with the warp and weft of place and voice — the place and voice of my childhood.

— Barry Moser
Hatfield, Massachusetts

PAINTINGS DONE IN TRANSPARENT WATERCOLOR ON HANDMADE PAPER
FROM THE HAYLE MILLS OF BARCHAM GREEN & COMPANY, LTD.,
MAIDSTONE, ENGLAND

COLOR SEPARATIONS MADE BY NEW INTERLITHO

TEXT COMPOSED IN MATTHEW CARTER'S GALLIARD IN 12-POINT SIZE
BY LITHO COMPOSITION COMPANY, INC., BOSTON, MASSACHUSETTS

ORIGINAL CALLIGRAPHY BY REASSURANCE WUNDER
OF HARLAN COUNTY, KENTUCKY

PRINTED AND BOUND BY NEW INTERLITHO